Get More Customers!

(Easy Online Techniques for Your Offline Business)

ED AKEHURST

Oak Publishing Group
Baltimore, MD

ISBN: 1456594273
ISBN-13: 978-1456594275

DEDICATION

This book is dedicated to Isvara, without whom this book would not exist, and to my wife and children, without whom I would never have had the inspiration to do the things I've done.

CONTENTS

Legal Notice

INTRODUCTION

Search Engine Optimization (SEO) is a topic within Internet and marketing circles that is much talked about and on which there is much speculation as to best practices. What can be agreed on is that even as an offline or brick-and-mortar business owner, it is imperative in this day and age that your business have a website, and that it be optimized for the search engines.

Whether you optimize your site yourself, or decide to use an in-house technician or outside consultant will depend greatly on the amount of time you are able to dedicate to it, your personal knowledge and experience and what goals you have for your website.

I have written this book to remove some of the mystique that surrounds SEO, and to guide you through some of the basic steps that will make a huge difference not only in the optimization of your site for search engines, but also to make sure your site is optimized for the best user experience. It is, after all, the visitors to your site that must be pleased and benefitted if you want any chance at all of converting them into paying customers.

After reading this book, I am sure you will agree that SEO work is crucial to the success of your online presence, and that your online presence can greatly impact your offline business. It is up to you whether you ultimately decide to do that SEO work yourself or you hire someone else to do it, but it is a decision that cannot be properly made without knowing what it is that needs to be done and having at least a basic understanding of the mechanics involved.

This book is not designed to be an in-depth course on mastering the fine art and science of SEO, but rather is geared towards pointing you in the right direction to make the most out of your website so that you may get more customers. At the end of the book, I will provide numerous resources so that if you choose to do the SEO work yourself, you will have reputable places to go to learn the ins and outs and be able to perform the work successfully.

If you choose to hire a SEO consultant or even a content writer (whose function can impact your site as much as, if not more than, an SEO expert), then you must know what it is they are supposed to do and how they ought to be doing it. Otherwise, you are just giving them a blank check with the sincere hope that they are honest and will not overcharge you.

In this book, we will show you what Search Engine Optimization is, and the ways in which it can be effectively used. We will provide you with the basics on using SEO to improve quality traffic flow to your site. The operative word here is "quality".

The quality of these visitors will often be measured by what specific keywords they are using in order to reach the desired result they want such as making a purchase, or it could just be viewing or downloading a particular page on that site. It may be that the visitor just requests some further information, or they sign up to a newsletter. Either way, you want them to find what they came looking for so that they will come back another time.

We will discuss the differences in keywords and how to arrive at those that will bring paying customers or at the very least, seriously interested ones that will return again and again.

Search Engine Optimization can be used as a marketing strategy that can often generate a good return for the site, and in turn for the business itself. However, there are many approaches to SEO, some more effective than others. Many SEO consultants try to beat the algorithms that the search engines use. The problem with this strategy is that those algorithms change from time to time, which means redesigning your site every time that happens. In that case, what you did last year or even last month may or may not be effective today.

The strategies we talk about in this book are known as "evergreen", meaning they are always effective - past, present and future. The reason for this is they are primarily geared towards human beings who will visit the site and secondarily towards the various search engines.

However, even if you do find that you have increased traffic to your site because of good SEO implementation, if your site is unprepared for this increased traffic it may in fact be detrimental, as your visitors will go away feeling dissatisfied and may not return. One way to help make sure they are satisfied and will return is through Site Optimization.

Site Optimization is about making sure the site layout is user friendly, that there are things of interest on the site for the visitors to peruse, that there is a reason to come back to the site, and that there is something to engage the visitor and inspire them to take some type of action. That could be anything from signing up for an email list, downloading some information, or planning a phone call or physical trip to the business that owns the site.

Remember the difference: Search Engine Optimization is used to get the visitor to the site, and Site Optimization is to get the visitor to feel glad they are there and to return. Proper Site Optimization will also assist with SEO.

Another topic we will address is the impact that off-site content publishing can have on a website. This is one of the major, yet often overlooked, keys to great SEO tactics. Offsite content publishing can be anything published that is not on the website of the business, from press releases to articles written about the business to related industry write-ups that reference the business. This aspect of SEO can make or break a website, and can have a huge impact on the business itself, including an impact on the foot traffic at a physical location.

If you have no intention of doing your own SEO, it is still in your best interest to take the time to absorb this information, as it will help you make the right decisions as to who to hire to do your SEO, Site Optimization and Media Publishing for your business. It will also assist you in making sure they are doing all that needs to be done and doing it in such a way that is of the greatest benefit to you.

- Ed Akehurst

SEO Consultant

Content Editor, Oak Publishing Group

Baltimore, MD

January, 2011

FOREWORD:
SEARCH ENGINES AND HOW THEY WORK

This section is designed for those who are not aware of how Search Engines relate to marketing on the Internet. If you have been marketing and advertising on the Internet for a while, feel free to skip to Chapter 1 or you may want to use the foreword as a review prior to digging in deeper. For everyone else, this section will lay the foundation for the rest of the information to come.

Search Engines are special sites on the Web that are designed to help people find information stored on other sites. There are differences in the way various Search Engines work, but they all perform three basic tasks:

- They search the Internet - or select pieces of the Internet - based on important words,
- They keep an index of the words they find, and where they find them, and
- They allow users to look for words or combinations of words found in that index.

Early Search Engines held an index of a few hundred thousand pages and documents, and received maybe one or two thousand inquiries each day. Today, a top Search Engine will index hundreds of millions of pages, and respond to tens of millions of queries per day.

11

Before a Search Engine can tell you where a file or document is, it must be found. To find information on the hundreds of millions of Web pages that exist, a Search Engine employs special software robots, called spiders, to build lists of the words found on Web sites.

When a spider is building its lists, the process is called web crawling.

In order to build and maintain a useful list of words, a Search Engine's spiders have to look at a lot of pages. How does any spider start its travels over the Web? The usual starting points are lists of heavily used servers and very popular pages. The spider will begin with a popular site, indexing the words on its pages and following every link found within the site. In this way, the spidering system quickly begins to travel, spreading out across the most widely used portions of the Web.

Once the spiders have completed the task of finding information on Web pages, the Search Engine must store the information in a way that makes it useful. There are two key components involved in making the gathered data accessible to users:

- The information stored with the data, and
- The method by which the information is indexed.

In the simplest case, a Search Engine could just store the word and the URL where it was found. In reality, this would make for an engine of limited use, since there would be no way of telling whether the word was used in an important or a trivial way on the page, whether the word was used once or many times or whether the page contained links to other pages containing the word. In other words, there would be no way of building the ranking list that tries to present the most useful pages at the top of the list of search results.

To make for more useful results, most Search Engines store more than just the word and URL. A Search Engine might store the number of times that the word appears on a page. The engine might assign a weight to each entry, with increasing values assigned to words as they appear near the top of the document, in sub-headings, in links, in the META tags or in the title of the page. Each commercial Search Engine has a different formula for assigning weight to the words in its index. This is one of the reasons that a search for the same word on different Search Engines will produce different lists, with the pages presented in different orders.

An index has a single purpose: it allows information to be found as quickly as possible. There are quite a few ways for an index to be built, but one of the most effective ways is to build a hash table. In hashing, a formula is applied to attach a numerical value to each word.

The formula is designed to evenly distribute the entries across a predetermined number of divisions. This numerical distribution is different from the distribution of words across the alphabet, and that is the key to a hash table's effectiveness.

When a person requests a search on a keyword or phrase, the Search Engine software searches the index for relevant information. The software then provides a report back to the searcher with the most relevant web pages listed first. The pages containing that report are called SERPs (Search Engine Results Pages).

CHAPTER 1
WHY USE SEO? WHAT ARE THE BEST PRACTICES?

INTRODUCTORY NOTE: If a section or even a chapter seems above your head or is unclear, please keep reading. It will all make more sense as you delve deeper into the book. I have also added a Glossary as Appendix E (page 58) if you encounter an unfamiliar term.

Search Engine Optimization (SEO) is crucial for the success of any web site. Unless people already have your URL (that is your web address, such as www.edakehurst.com) they need a way to find your site. You can buy ads, you can use Pay Per Click advertising, you can hand out business cards, or any of hundreds of other creative ways. There are many ways to get the word out about your site.

With SEO, though, you can be found in the search engines, such as Google and Yahoo! If you own a cupcake store and sell, for example, cupcake tins, you would want to be found online by people searching for cupcake tins. You want your site to be optimized in such a way that when someone types "cupcake tins" into a search engine, your site is one of the first ones they find.

A well-ranked site will be near the top of the listings. That is the goal of SEO: to find the phrases that people are searching for and have your site be on that first page when they run their search.

Unfortunately, there are no shortcuts to getting your site well ranked. If you are looking for a way to get quick and easy results without any effort, then this isn't it. You will need to carry out some hard work (or pay someone to carry it out for you), especially in relation to the actual content on your site and related to your site.

It also helps to have plenty of patience, as results do not usually happen overnight. In light of that fact, when looking to improve the search engine position of your site you need to take action sooner rather than later. Sometimes results can be seen in days, but sometimes it can take weeks or months, it just depends on the nature of your business, how well optimized your competition is, and what it is you would like to accomplish.

However, even though sooner is better, it is imperative to do it correctly with an actual plan in mind. It is quite possible for haphazard SEO that does not have a proper foundation or game plan to do more damage than good.

Some of the following strategies and tips deal with Search Engine Optimization, and some with Site Optimization, but as you will begin to see the two go hand in hand.

Good Content, On and Off Site

Although your site may be set up to be technically perfect for the search engine robots to find it, you will find few if any benefits to your business if the actual content of your site is not relevant, well-written and properly presented. This is probably the single most important point you should remember when doing SEO (or having SEO done), especially if you want your site to be found on the web by visitors that will convert to paying customers.

Regardless of what your site is about, the content needs to be unique, specific and helpful in order to appeal to people. Moreover, to have an actual impact on your business, it needs to be particularly appealing to those people looking specifically for information about your products or services.

In other words, if the visitor searched for "best cupcake tins", but your site offers cupcake recipes for sale, they will certainly have an interest in your topic, but that is not what is on their mind at the moment they come to your site. They will leave and possibly never come back. They will keep looking for cupcake tins, and later, when they are actually searching for cupcake recipes, they may or may not remember that your site is there.

This does not mean that you should not offer cupcake recipes. It simply means if you are optimized for "best cupcake tins", be sure there is relevant content there for the visitor to find when they arrive (and hopefully a way for them to buy them, be it through an affiliate link or through your business). If there is, you have a chance of them bookmarking your site and coming back again and again.

Never forget, even when in full "SEO mode", the only reason we are attempting to drive traffic to your site is to please visitors so they stay a while and hopefully come back. That, in turn, is only important, because we want at some point to convert them to paying customers. This book is not about theory – it is about how to Get More Customers! Never lose sight of that fact.

Inbound Links

By having great, relevant content on (and off) your site, visitors will return and some of those visitors who return will want to link their information to your site. These are called "inbound links". For example, if I visit your site about cupcake recipes that you sell, and I like it enough to go back to my Baking Blog and put up a link directing my readers to your site, I have given you an inbound link.

Having lots of quality inbound links is not only great for your site, but for search engine rankings also. It is even better if those links are from sites that rank higher in the search engines than your own. We will cover this in greater depth in later chapters.

Not only do you need to have good, relevant content on your site, you also need to have fresh content. If you add new content to your site on a regular basis, you are giving your visitors much more of a reason to return to it. Because of the constantly changing content, search engine robots will also visit your site more often. What this means for you is that any new content you add, will then be indexed in the search engines much more quickly in the future.

This goes for constantly updated off-site content as well, although we will go into that in much more detail later.

Check your Spellings, and use Site-Appropriate Grammar

Take the time to make sure you are not committing spelling errors. There is nothing more amateurish than typos and misspellings on your site.

Additionally, you are probably aware of the differences in spelling between American and British English. Where in the UK they will write, "colour", in the USA it is written as "color", and the same can be said of "optimisation" and "optimization". Make sure the spelling style matches your target audience.

Grammar is handled a little differently. If your business is investments, for example, and you need a very professional image, you will want to use very formal grammar, whereas if your business is selling Rock and Roll T-Shirts, your grammar would need to be colloquial and loose. A word such as "ain't" would not prudently show up on a website for a bank, but is perfectly acceptable on a page selling shoes for teenagers.

A lot of this really boils down to knowing your target audience. Take the same skillset and logic you would use in designing your store displays or newspaper ads and apply it to your website.

Make sure your Page Titles are Descriptive

If you make your page titles as simple, descriptive and relevant as possible, it will make it easier for the search engines to know what each page of your site is about. This will allow people to scan through the search results they get, and be able to quickly determine if your web site contains what they are actually looking for. Also, it should be remembered that the page title is what is used as the link to your site from the results provided by the search engines. Google shows these as blue underlined text.

Because of this, you need to make certain that the title on the page is one of your most relevant elements of your site. Some people will argue that this the most important part of any site above all other things. My personal opinion is that while it may not be the most important part, it definitely has importance and needs to be treated accordingly. See more Title Tag information on page 28.

Use of Real Text Headings and Headers

In the header of a web site, many people use graphical text instead of real text. If you are not sure which your site has, try to highlight the text with your mouse, by holding down the button and dragging the cursor over the text. If it will not highlight, it is most likely a graphic. By using graphics for your headings you are able to use any typeface you want, but search engines will not pay much attention to this.

Even if you use an alt attribute text with the graphic, which is where you can assign a text phrase to a picture for the search engine robots to read, this is not anywhere near as powerful as using real text in a heading element.

Most HTML editors (as well as word processing editors) will have styles known as "header". They range from h1 to h6. The largest, known as an h1 tag, is what should be used in page headers to get the most recognition from search engines. See page 29 for more information.

If you are unable to use real text, then be sure to use an alt text with the image, and make sure it is just as relevant to the page as if you were writing a heading.

Be Sure that your URLs are Search Engine Friendly

It is important to use search engine friendly URLs, as opposed to dynamically generated ones that have a query string (which lets the server know which data to fetch from a database). There are many search engine robots that have difficulties with dynamic URLs. They may well stop at the question mark, and therefore will not actually look at the query string. Dynamic URL looks like this: www.cupcakes.com/search?cupcakes and shows that the term after the question mark, in this cake "cupcakes", was used to dynamically generate the page.

If the previous paragraph is beyond your expertise at the moment, what is important for you to be sure of is that the specific URL of every page on your site that you would like to for rank never changes. For SEO purposes, it needs to be static, rather than dynamic. There are reasons for a dynamic page name, which usually deal with displaying results from a database query, but for most purposes, and for the purposes of any page that you will want to optimize for search engine ranking, this will never be a need.

By using search engine friendly URLs you are helping not only your ranking, but also the users of your site. Many sites have seen an incredible improvement just because they have changed the URL scheme on it from dynamic to static.

The URL should also be keyword-relevant, so that it "fits" the rest of the page.

Getting Linked

The best way for your site to be certain it gets linked from other sites is to have good, relevant content. For any site on the web, incoming links are very important, especially for Search Engine Optimization. Getting other people to link to your site can sometimes be a challenge. There is no quick and easy or sustainable way to solve this without offsite media publishing.

For many, they find that this is the hardest part of SEO to implement. There are many people who specialize in getting links, but there are good ways of doing it and ways that will come back to haunt you. I have dedicated an entire chapter to this later in the book.

Some people have claimed that incoming links are less important where there is more specific and unique content on the site. This may have some merit, but there is no doubt that lots of relevant links will significantly enhance a web site's ranking.

Make it Accessible to All

Accessibility involves, among other things, having text alternatives to audio and visual information on a page, as well as making sure that links can be navigated by keyboard only and font sizes can be maximized while maintaining site integrity.

This can be more important than most people are willing to admit. It can affect search engine results to a degree, but it can also greatly improve a visitor's experience on the site. You will at the very least want to make your site accessible to those who are visually impaired, as this will help search engine robots find their way around it also. It is important to remember that the search engine robots are "blind", so even if you are not bothered whether blind people use your site or not (which we all should be in today's world); you still need for it to be accessible. What this means is that you should use real text headings, paragraphs and lists, and avoid using anything that may interfere with the search engine spiders.

Be Careful when Making a Submission

Although this is often overrated, submitting your site to directories and search engines can actually be useful. This is especially important if the site happens to be new and has not yet been picked up by Google or many of the other search engines.

The problem can arise when you submit to too many engines or directories too quickly. It looks unnatural to the engines and can create a situation where you get de-ranked for attempting to manipulate the algorithms.

You definitely want to submit your site to some directories, but be sure to do only a few at a time. You may want to consider using Yahoo Directory and DMOZ Open Directory Project and some directories specific to your topic (for example, if you have a blog, you can try submitting to http://www.blog-search.info). But you will need patience, as it can take several weeks for submissions to some of these directories to be processed unless you pay for it to be listed.

Do Not Try to Fool the Search Engines

Never use such methods as cloaking, link farms, keyword stuffing, alt text spamming or any other dubious ways of attempting to manipulate the search engines. Although some of these techniques may work for a short time, you not only risk getting your site penalized, but it could actually be banned from some search engines altogether.

Search engine companies strive for their results to be as accurate as possible. They do not take kindly to people trying to trick them.

If you are hiring someone to do SEO, make sure they are not using these types of tactics on your site. The same goes for hiring Media and Content Publishers. If they submit articles with links back to your site, you want those articles to be readable and relevant to your visitors, and not artificially stuffed with keywords. You also want them on reputable sites and sites that are as relevant to the topic of your site as possible.

Avoid the Use of Frames

Although it is possible to provide workarounds that will allow a search engine robot to crawl frame-based sites, these can still cause problems for any visitors who find that site through a search engine.

What happens is that when someone follows a link from a search result to a frame-based site, they will end up on an orphaned document. This will, in many cases, create confusion for the user, as vital parts of the site could be lost, such as navigational links.

In most instances, it is just not necessary to use frames.

Browser Detection – Be Careful

If you have to use some kind of browser detection, then make sure that it does not break when a search engine spider or any other unknown agent comes along. Unfortunately, if the spiders cannot get in, then your site will not be found and will not get indexed.

Meta Tags – Myth or Meaningful?

A Meta Tag is a piece of information about your site that cannot be seen by the visitor, but can be seen by the search engines. You will find that most search engines today do not seem to place a great deal of value on the content contained within Meta Tags. This is because spammers have overused them too frequently in the past. With that said, it does not hurt to fill some of them in.

Keep in mind that the Title Element is not actually a Meta Tag – it needs to be there.

I recommend using the Meta Description Tag, as some search engines still use that as the description in the search result listings. It can be beneficial to the people searching so they can see the relevancy of the page they have found. Whenever possible, make the description contents unique and descriptive for every page. Keep in mind, though, that the search engines cut these off in the results at around 160 characters, so a person viewing the results may not see anything beyond that.

Although the Meta Keywords Tag does not have a huge impact, it does have some in at least a couple of the major search engines, so take the time to enter some of the relevant keywords from the page (just don't over do it – a handful of keywords is more than enough).

We will take a more in-depth look at Meta Tags in the next chapter.

As stated at the beginning of this chapter, we are providing a few basic guidelines in relation to SEO. Be aware that there is much more that can be done in order to increase your site's visibility with search engines. A good SEO consultant can do wonders for your site.

Which begs the question: Is it more beneficial to do SEO yourself or to hire someone?

As a Media and Content Publisher and an SEO consultant, I would surely love it if everyone decided to pay for my services, but the fact is that is not always the wise thing for a business to do. SEO work is very time consuming and therefore can get a bit on the expensive side if there is a lot of optimization to do or a lot of content to add (not all SEO consultants do content).

A business owner needs to weigh the amount of time they can afford to spend away from their primary business doing SEO versus the cost of hiring a consultant.

Rarely does it make sense for a small business to outsource all of their SEO work. However, a small business owner (or even a mid-sized business owner) can do some of the basics themselves, and then have a consultant come in to tweak the site and make sure it has a competitive edge.

A qualified SEO consultant can also do other things that have not been mentioned here, such as optimizing for Google Places and integrating social media such as a Facebook or Twitter page.

Media and Content Publishing, which is much different than SEO, can be extremely time consuming and is a very specialized skill. In many cases it makes sense for that to be the outsource priority over SEO work. A good Media and Content Publisher can have a huge impact on a site's ranking and can potentially get a much better bang for the buck than targeted ads in the print media.

In chapter 5, we will discuss Media and Content Publishing in more depth and show how it can make a positive impact on your site, which will in turn drive business to your store and help you get more customers.

CHAPTER 2
SET UP THE BASIC LINK STRUCTIRE
WITHIN A SITE

What is link structure?

What we are referring to is actually internal link structure, and this is how different pages within your site are laid out and how they correlate to each other. We will also discuss various Meta Tags as well, since they are related to some degree.

Link structure is probably one of the most overlooked aspects of Search Engine Optimization. It helps to make sure that search engine spiders can actually find (crawl) all of your site's pages, and it also shows relevance within a site. By that, I mean there is not one page on cupcakes, one on motorcycles, and another on acoustic guitars.

If your link structure is not well optimized, you are not only making it more difficult for the search engines to see each page, you are leaving in doubt how relevant your pages are to each other. If the search engine spiders cannot find all of your relevant pages, then they won't get indexed. If that happens, no amount of Search Engine Optimization will help.

In this chapter, we will cover some points that should be taken into serious consideration when designing and optimizing the link structure of your site.

Spiders cannot easily see links that are accomplished by JavaScript. This is changing, but the technology is not quite there yet, so while it might not be impossible for a spider to crawl a dynamic link or a JavaScript link, it is very difficult and you are severely reducing your chances of having pages indexed that are linked that way. If you want spiders to follow the links on your site, do not use JavaScript. HTML (HyperText Markup Language) is the standard language that web pages are written in and is best for maximum search engine "crawlability".

It is important that you make sure all pages link to at least one other relevant page. Pages that do not link out to another page are known as "dangling links".

It is not advisable for links to go more than three "levels" deep. The structure of a site should not be such that many levels are required. For example, in a cupcake web site, the main links might go to recipes, equipment, ingredients, pictures, and a blog. We'll call these "Level 1". Each of these might have sub-topics. Equipment might have a page on baking tins, a page on cupcake wrappers, and a page on cupcake picks. These pages would be known as "Level 2". Tins might have sub-pages about different sizes and styles of tins. These would be "Level 3" pages.

Of equal importance is for links (internal and external) to be structured in such a way that targeted search terms are reinforced.

For example, a website for a cupcake store has different pages on different topics. Other than the common navigation menu, we want to link them together in various ways (without overdoing it).

On a page with cupcake recipes, there would be a link to a specific recipe. The name of the recipe will be the link text, i.e. the recipe name will be the actual clickable link.

That link shows relevance, it "highlights" one of the keywords for the recipe page, and it makes sense for the visitor. On the page with the recipe, there could be a recommended cupcake tin size and type, perhaps a six-cavity popover pan. The phrase "six-cavity popover pan" would be the actual clickable link (link text), linking to a page dedicated to six-cavity popover pans, their features, some pictures and a mention of the fact that your cupcake store sells them.

Here are some methods using HTML to accomplish the above, as well as related optimization techniques. If you are unsure what these are used for, you can acquire the assistance of a web designer or a SEO professional to help you properly implement these.

Link Text:

<a href="http://cupcake.com/tins">cupcake tins</a>

Link text is one of the two most important elements to ensure good rankings for a site, the other being the Title Tag. It can be used on linked pages within the site, or on backlinks to the site's pages, especially internal pages. It is important that it is done in this way, so that the actual words ("cupcake tins" in the example for this sub section) are the link itself. It is best if you use the target page's main search term in the link text, especially from an internal link.

If there are several links pointing to that page (from external sites, there will hopefully be many of them, perhaps hundreds), do not use identical text for every link that links to a page. You can target many different keywords by varying the link text on each of these links.

Links will carry more weight with search engines the more relevant the link text is to the target page's main topic and relevant search terms (keywords).

Title Tag:

<title>6 Cavity Popover Cupcake Pans</title>

The Title Tag is possibly the second most important page element in order to get good rankings for a site. It is important that the page's main search term is contained within this tag. Place the keyword as near to the front as possible while ensuring that the title reads well on the page.

There is nothing wrong with placing the search term up front on its own and then following it with a period. If the search term is "6 Cavity Popover Cupcake Pans", the Title Tag and page heading could be, "6 Cavity Popover Cupcake Pans. Which One Is The Best?"

Make sure that each page's Title Tag is different from the title tags on your site's other pages. Each page should be relevant, but unique.

Description Tag:

<meta name="description" content="Information and pricing on cupcake tins.">

You will find that some search engines, such as Google, do not always display the description in the same way as they have in the past. However, it is recommended that you include this on each page for the search engines that do still display them that way.

It is vital that you write a description that is appealing to the potential visitor and at the same time incorporates the page's main search term into it at least once and preferably near or at the beginning. It needs to read naturally, and should reflect the actual content of the page.

Keywords Tag:

<meta="keywords" content="cupcakes, baking">

It is important to remember that the content within the Keywords

Tag is never actually treated by search engines as keywords. They will be treated as text on a page. Although this tag is not nearly as effective as it used to be, there is no reason to leave it out. Instead, make sure that you put in several relevant keywords and include the main search term once at the front of the tag. Separate each keyword or keyword phrase with commas and do not do what is known as "keyword stuffing". Keyword stuffing is where you add many keywords for the express purpose of trying to attract the attention of a search engine. Using a lot of keywords, or keywords that do not match the content of the page can cause the site to get flagged as spam.

H Tag:

<Hn>Cupcake Recipes</Hn>

The "n" in this tag represents a number from 1 to 6. H1 represents the largest sized heading. You will find that H tags are given more weight than ordinary text in a page, and so the bigger the H size, the more weight it will have. So it is important that you include your target search term in the H tags at least once on the page, but if possible two or three times is even better, so long as it follows a natural reading flow and is not there just to throw in extra keywords. It is also helpful to place your first H Tag as near to the top of the site page as possible.

Bold Text:

Bold text gives more weight to a page than ordinary text, but not as much as an H Tag does. Occasionally, if it can appear natural, enclose the search term in bold tags where it appears on the page. Again, do not overdo this or it will be considered spamming.

Normal Text:

The main search term should appear about once every hundred words, or maybe a little more, so that the density of the word compared to the total number of words is about 1%. The keywords ought not detract from how the page actually reads.

You can use the main search term once or twice in the very early pages of the body text, and then sprinkled lightly throughout. If you need to, you can rewrite content to make sure the search term is properly represented in the text for good SEO and Site Optimization.

You also want to add other relevant keywords throughout, especially ones that can be used as link text to other pages within the site.

Alt Text:

<img src="cupcake.com" alt="cupcake">

Alt Text is an alternative word where a graphic image appears that can be used for accessibility by visually impaired people and as a text replacement. Systems such as those used by Braille readers and speech synthesizers use the Alt Text. Include your relevant search term in the Alt Text of all images on your pages.

Summary:

1.   Select the main search terms you wish to use.

2.   Allocate these search terms to a suitable existing page, and if you need to, split pages.

3.   Organize your internal links, using link text to match the target search terms and their respective pages.

4.   If you can, organize those links from other pages to suit the target search terms and their pages also.

5.   Now organize all the on-page elements so that they fit each page's target search term.

6.   Finally, sit back and watch your page rankings begin to improve.

CHAPTER 3
EFFECTIVE USE OF KEYWORDS FOR SEO

Selecting Search Engine Keywords

Your keywords serve as the foundation of your online marketing strategy. If they are not chosen with great precision, no matter how aggressive your marketing campaign may be, the right people may never get the chance to find out about what you offer. To avoid obscurity, your first step in implementing your strategy is to gather and evaluate appropriate keywords and phrases.

You may think you know the right words for your search phrases right off the top of your head. Unfortunately, in many cases you would be wrong. There are certain steps that must be followed to ensure that your keywords exactly match what your potential customers are typing into the search engines to find what you have to offer. Otherwise, you are just guessing at what those words might be. If you are off even by even a small margin, your customers will find your competition instead.

It's hard to be objective when you are right in the center of your business network, which is one of the reasons you may not be able to choose the most efficient keywords off the top of your head. You need to be able to think like your customers, and since you are a business owner and not the consumer, your best strategy is two-fold. You need to go directly to the source (customers in your niche), and you need to properly research the keywords you find to make sure they are being used and they are commercially viable.

To accurately identify the appropriate keywords, ask for words from as many potential customers as you can find. You will usually discover that the understanding you have of your business is significantly different from your customers' understanding.

The consumer is an invaluable resource. You will find that the words you accumulate from them are words and phrases you probably never would have considered without looking at your business from the consumer's perspective.

There are numerous ways to gather these words and phrases from the consumer. One is to poll your customers when they come to the store. You can also offer to have them complete an online survey in exchange for something such as a coupon.

Ask them what they like best about the store, about your website, about the products you carry. Ask them directly how they found you and what they searched for to find you on the web.

Forums

Another way is to visit forums on the Internet. There are several websites that you can use to find web forums in your niche market:

- Big-Boards.com
- Omgili.com
- ForumVirus.com
- BoardReader.com

There are others, but those are the main ones. You can also go to Google and type in some searches looking for forums about your niche. You would type your industry and then words to help you find the forums. In the cupcake business for example, you could use any of the following searches to find boards or forums:

- Cupcake forums
- Cupcake message boards
- Baking forums
- Baking message boards

Once you click through to some of the message boards and forums, you are looking for words and phrases that people are using and discussing. This identifies the hot topics at the moment and can help you get into the mind of the consumer. As a business owner, you might think the consumer is looking for "cheapest cupcake tin" when really they are looking for "nonstick cupcake tin" and the price is not as much of an issue.

Many of the searches carried out on the net contain three words or more (we call these "long tail keywords"). When people are searching for answers on the Internet, they will often phrase their search term as a question. Many people will not use search words that describe the solution to a question. In order to optimize your pages to their full extent, you must think like the person who is searching.

Without directly asking the customers and without looking through their discussions with each other on forums and message boards, you would only be guessing as to which words and phrases they would actually use to find you on the web, and you would never come up with the long tail keywords.

Research your Competition

You can also add to your list of keywords by checking out the competition. This can be a great way of getting keyword ideas, especially if the competitor's site is well optimized, meaning they have already done a lot of the keyword research.

Take some of the terms that you would like to target and enter them into Google. Click through to each of the top sites that come up as a result of this search. Once on the site, view their source HTML code and view the keywords that they have in their Meta tags. To view a sites HTML code, all you do is click on the "View" button at the top of your web browser page and then select "Source" or "Page Source". Any keywords they are using that relate to your business can be added to your list (you still want to do your own due diligence on the keywords).

Only after you have gathered a good amount of words and phrases from outside resources should you add your own keywords to the list. Come up with as many relevant phrases as possible. It is beneficial if your list has at least 40 or 50 keywords or phrases. Once you have this list in hand, you are ready for the next step.

Evaluation

The aim of evaluation is to narrow down your list to a small number of very specific words and phrases that will direct the highest number of quality visitors to your website. By "quality visitors" I mean those consumers who are most likely to make a purchase rather than just cruise around your site and take off for greener pastures. In evaluating the effectiveness of keywords, bear in mind three elements: popularity, specificity, and motivation.

Popularity is the easiest to evaluate, because it is an objective quality. The more popular your keyword is, the more likely the chances are that it will be typed into a Search Engine which could then bring up your URL.

There is software on the market that will rate the popularity of keywords and phrases based on several factors of real Search Engine activity. Some such software will even suggest variations on your words and phrases. Variations are important, because even a subtle difference can have an impact. The phrase "cupcake baking tins" has completely different search results than "baking cupcake tins". The more popular a given keyword, the more traffic you can logically expect to be able to be directed to your site.

The only problem with using only this concept is the more popular the keyword is, the greater the Search Engine position you will need to obtain. If you are down at the bottom of the search results, the consumer will probably never page through to find you.

Popularity isn't enough to declare a keyword a good choice. You must also consider the next criteria, which is specificity. The more specific your keyword is, the greater the likelihood that the consumer who is ready to purchase your goods or services will find you.

Let's look at a hypothetical example. Imagine that you have obtained popularity rankings for the keyword "baking" However, your company specializes in cupcakes only. The keyword "cupcake stores" would rank lower on the popularity scale than "baking" but it would nevertheless serve you much better.

Instead of getting a lot of people directed to your site who are interested in everything from buying the right oven to learning how to apply icing to a cake, you will get only those looking for cupcake related items and information. In other words, consumers ready to buy your specific services are the ones who will immediately find you.

Not only that, but the greater the specificity of your keyword is, the less competition you will face. For example, if your cupcake store is in Baltimore, the phrase "Baltimore cupcake store" will certainly have less competition than the more generic phrase "cupcake store".

The third factor is consumer motivation. Once again, this requires putting yourself inside the mind of the customer rather than the seller to figure out what motivation prompts a person looking for a service or product to type in a particular word or phrase.

Let's look at another example, such as a consumer who is specifically searching for a nonstick carbon steel cupcake tin. If you have to choose between the keyword phrases "cupcake tin" and "nonstick carbon steel cupcake tin," which do you think will benefit the consumer more? If you were looking for this specific type of tin, which keyword would you type in? The second one, of course!

Using the second keyword targets people who have already decided on what they want, have already done some of the research, and are more likely ready to buy a product than someone just generally searching for tins. The second one is much farther along the buying process.

You want to find people who are more ready to act or are closer to making a purchase. This requires subtle tinkering with your keywords until you find the most specific and directly targeted phrases to bring the most motivated traffic to your site, and ultimately to your store itself.

Once you have chosen your keywords, your work is not done. You must continually evaluate performance across a variety of Search Engines, bearing in mind that times and trends change, as does popular lingo. You cannot rely on analyzing your log of website traffic alone because it will not tell you how many of your visitors actually made a purchase, or how many made the physical trip to your store.

Fortunately, there are tools available to help you judge the effectiveness of your keywords. There are also people such as myself who can provide this information to you on an ongoing basis. That can help you discern which keywords have the potential to bring you the most valuable customers.

You want to find keywords that direct consumers to your site who actually buy your product, fill out your forms, get on your mailing list, or visit your store. This is the most important factor in evaluating the efficacy of a keyword or phrase and should be your main motivation when weeding out ineffective or inefficient keywords with keywords that will bring in better profits.

Ongoing analysis of tested keywords is the formula for Search Engine success. This may sound like a lot of work - and it is! But the amount of informed effort you put into your keyword campaign is what will ultimately generate your business' rewards. If you do not have the time or the skills to do this, it might be better to pay someone to perform these functions. It is, however, important that you know what they are doing (and why) so you can make sure your SEO expenses are not going to waste.

Remember that while SEO is a lot of work, it does not need to be complicated. What you can do is make sure that each and every page of your site is a unique entity, and is treated in the appropriate manner where SEO is concerned. You need to make sure that the well-researched keywords are being properly and appropriately used, both within and without your site.

Once you have your list of viable keywords, here are some ways to make sure they are being properly used:

Include Keywords in your Page Titles

Unfortunately, a lot of people will use either inappropriate names or only their company name in the page titles. Be sure to include the appropriate keywords in your title, as that is they way people carry out searches on the Internet. This is also where you would use the h1 Tag for proper Site Optimization, matching and staying relevant with the other content and optimization on that page.

Inclusion of Keywords in your Title Tags and Meta Tags

It is vital that, for each page of your site, you include the appropriate keywords within all the page tags. Also, take time to go over the Meta Description Tag that you use. You should make sure that any description you use is alluring and interesting to those who are visiting your site. It needs to include keywords within it wherever possible without damaging readability. There are many search engines around today which use the Meta Description for the language that will be displayed in their search results.

Keywords in Page Content

It is important that you make sure you include keywords in the content of your site as well. Just don't over do this, as too many will result in your page being discounted by the search engines. Each page will have a main keyword, but also will have several related keywords. These will become anchor links (link text) to other pages on the site that use the related keywords as their main keyword.

Keywords in Offsite Content

Offsite content can be a huge boon to your site. This includes articles, press releases, blogs, event calendars, and map listings, among others. A good Media and Content Publisher can not only implement much of this properly, but they are usually much more effective and less expensive than other forms of marketing and advertising.

Using these basic guidelines, you will find that your site cannot help but be affected in a positive way.

If your site is already built, you may be thinking that it is too late to select your keywords. It's not! It does not matter if you choose your keywords before or after the site has gone live (although it is better to do it before, as then you will not need to rewrite the text on the pages). If your site is live, pages can always be edited, added or even deleted. What is important is that each page is reaching its full optimization value. By using a thorough keyword selection process, you can make sure that the keywords you are using are optimized to their fullest extent, and the pages are implementing them in the best possible way.

CHAPTER 4
SEARCH ENGINE FRIENDLY CONTENT TO BOOST YOUR SITE

In this chapter, we will look at what search engine friendly content is and how to use it to boost your site. Although many people think it is about stuffing your website with targeted keywords, it isn't. In fact, you may find that you could seriously damage your search engine rankings if you do this.

What you need is to write copy (or have someone write copy for you) that will be looked at not only by search engine spiders, but also by human beings. There is no point in having a site that is highly ranked if none of the visitors can understand or appreciate it. Your site must be user friendly both to your visitors and the search engine spiders.

First of all you need to answer the following questions:

- What is the purpose of your site?
- What do you want your visitors to do when they reach it?
- Would you like them to spend money when they arrive?
- Do you just want to provide them with information?
- Do you want them to sign up for an email list?

These are important to remember when writing content for your site, as the answer to these questions need to impact that content.

Whenever possible, use short paragraphs or bullet points. These are much more likely to attract and retain visitors, while more lengthy essay-looking pages tend to drive them away.

If you are selling a service or product then you need to make your site look interesting. Provide as many calls to action as you can. Do not just provide them with an online price list. People want information presented in an engaging way. You can also include pictures and/or video, if appropriate.

Entice the visitors to provide you with their contact information. If you sell cupcakes at your store, you could "bribe" them to sign up for your email list by offering them a 10% off coupon or even a free sample, or perhaps the purpose of the list could be so they can be notified before the general public when your products will be going on sale.

Never lose sight of the fact that even though you are trying to attract the search engines, your site should be designed first and foremost for human readers. As long as a site has been designed well with people in mind, then more likely than not you will find that it is also well on the way to being search engine friendly.

When a search engine is looking at your page, one of the things it is looking for is keyword phrases in your copy. Humans do too, without realizing it. They are always subconsciously checking to make sure they are being presented with information that is relevant to their likes and needs. You need to be a little more creative for humans and a little more formulaic for search engines. The perfect blend of those two is where the art of SEO comes in.

Here are some tips that if implemented properly will help in your SEO by using the content on your site in a way that the Search Engines appreciate:

1. Have at least 200 words of copy on each page of your site. Although this may be difficult at times, it is important so that the search engines do not think it is a spammy page. Remember that humans do not always appreciate long articles. Staying under 1,000 words on a page is also a good idea, unless it cannot be avoided.

2. This text, wherever possible, should include your most important keyword phrases, but should still remain logical and easy to read by visitors to the site. Do not keyword stuff. Use them naturally about one keyword every 75-100 words.

3. Use phrases that you have used in the other tags on the pages during this part of the optimization process. This shows theme relevancy, which means every page is relevant to the other pages on the site.

4. Add additional content filled pages to the site, such as how-to articles, tips or tutorials. These types of pages help with SEO, and provide the added benefit that other sites may link to yours. It also gives the visitors more reason to stay longer on your site, and to come back more frequently.

Search Engine Friendly Content is a specialty and is one area that is usually prudent to outsource, so long as you know what it is the content publisher is supposed to be providing you, and what to look for to make sure they are doing an excellent job.

The following services need to be provided, whether you hire a good Media and Content Publisher or you do it yourself:

- Market Research
- Keyword Development
- Related Keyword Development
- Page Topic Suggestions
- On Site Content
- Off Site Content (Articles and Press Releases)
- Distribution

You will also want to use social media, forums and blog posts, but these are usually best if done by you personally or by a designated in-house worker. For example, if you have a Facebook Fan Page (you do, don't you?) it can be beneficial to have one of the workers that sees customers every day add posts, as the customers know them and speak with them and already have a great relationship. Industry blogs and forums you can post to yourself.

See Chapter 6 for some tips on setting up a Facebook Business Page.

CHAPTER 5
USING CONTENT FOR BACKLINKS TO HELP WITH SEO

A backlink is a link that directs people to your site; they are also often referred to as inbound links. The number of backlinks that your site has can be an indication of how popular or important it is according to your peers (other site owners).

These are especially important for SEO, as search engines such as Google will give more credit to those sites with a good number of quality backlinks. They will consider these sites more relevant than others and give them better positioning in the results pages of a search query.

Most search engines will give a higher rank to those websites that humans actually find interesting. One way for them to identify this is to look for natural links that have been built slowly over time in different, but related areas of interest, as that is how the word of mouth about a site usually spreads.

Although it can be fairly easy to manipulate the links on a web page in order to achieve a higher ranking, it is a lot harder to influence a search engine with external backlinks from another site. This is why backlinks feature so highly in a search engine's algorithm.

It has become even harder today to achieve these quality inbound links because of unscrupulous webmasters. Such people try to acquire backlinks by deceptive or sneaky techniques through either hidden links or through automatically generated pages.

Some webmasters will also get links from sites that will link anyone, regardless of content or topic. Such pages are known as link farms and search engines generally disregard them. If you are using link farms for backlinks, you may find your site being ranked lower or possibly even banned entirely from some search engines.

Links ought to come primarily from sites that are very relevant to yours. It is best if they come from a relevant site with a higher Page Rank than yours (see the Glossary if this is a new term for you).

There are a number of ways in which backlinking can be legitimately achieved. One such way of achieving quality backlinks to a site is to entice quality visitors to come to your site by providing quality content relevant to your industry. Other ways are listed below.

Reciprocal Linking

This is where you link to another site that provides the same service or product as you and they in turn have a link to your site on theirs. The search engines do not give these the highest ratings, but as long as it is not a link farm you are doing this with it should be fine.

A better way to do this would be to link to site A, who links to site B, who links back to you. This is still not as good as a "one way" link going to you, but it can help nonetheless.

Site Submissions

Submit links for your site to website directories which allow free website submissions, or if your budget allows it, to some paid directories.

Be sure the sites you are submitting to are as relevant as possible. You will not get much search engine love by submitting your cupcake site to an automotive directory.

I have included a list of some of the best directories in the appendix.

Be aware that there are many sites which offer a service where you can submit your site details to numerous website directories at once. With only a few exceptions, this is not the best way to get listed, as it can appear unnatural and can get your site onto many directories that have little to no relevance. If you have an SEO consultant, have them help you decide whether using an automated directory listing service is advisable in your situation, as this will vary from business to business.

Articles

Getting articles published can be among the very best ways of getting great backlinks. It is vital that any articles you write are on topic, informative and thorough in relation to your site. I have included in the appendix some of the best article directories. This is an area that can make or break a site.

If an article about your business, or about your industry with a reference to your business, is posted online, that will give you an inbound link. If there are several such postings on a regular basis, it tends to give more weight to your site as being an authority.

Keep in mind that general articles about your industry will tend to get a larger readership than ones specifically about your business. If your business is listed in a resource box at the end of such an article, it then gives the appearance that your business is the industry authority on that topic. This can have great short and long term benefits to you.

A good Media and Content Publisher can handle this for you and is generally much cheaper and can get much better results than other forms of "advertising". These articles stay up forever and can, over time, greatly increase search engine rankings if done right. It is a true art form, and there are many things that must be in place for this to be effective. When done properly, they can set your business apart from the competition and help take you to the next level.

Here are just a few of the things to consider in order to write good articles for your site in such a way that you will get effective backlinks:

1. Write in a way that your intended target audience will understand what you are trying to say. In other words, don't write it like you were a teacher talking to a class of ten-year olds, but at the same time don't be overly complicated.

2. Have excellent spelling, grammar and punctuation. If in doubt, have them edited for you.

3. Do not make your article too long. Usually, a good article designed for both reader attention span and search engine love will have between 350 to 500 words.

4. The article must be newsworthy or informative, and not a sales pitch or an advertisement.

5. Always include a resource box at the end. On some of the better article sites, this will be the only place that you can have that all-important backlink to your site. This resource box should also include a short biography regarding you and/or your site. There are entire courses available on the best ways to treat a resource box. This is the heart of the backlinking strategy for many sites.

Blogging
This has now become an integral part of the Internet, and is one of the more effective ways of linking. You either have the choice of placing a few words of comments on to someone else's blog, or you may want to link to them from your own blog.

When adding comments to someone else's blog, you want to be able to link to your website from your name or occasionally from the post. You will use an optimized tag (link text) as your name. Instead of "John," which is not a good tag for a link to your cupcake site, you could use "Cupcake Baker."

If you update your blog regularly with interesting content, you will find that many blogs will be happy to give a link back to your site.

You can also consider guest blogging. This is where you go to a webmaster with a blog about your industry and offer to write an article that they can post on their site. Bloggers are always looking for good, relevant content. You will, in addition to being presented as an expert on the topic, be given a link back to your website.

Press Releases

Press releases are another great way to get backlinks. You must make sure they are newsworthy, and not a sales pitch. For example, you can do a press release if you introduce a new product. Just be sure the release is about the product and its impact on the marketplace or the benefits to the users and demonstrate that the introduction of such a product is newsworthy. At the end of the release you can mention the product is now available at your business.

Press release writing can be an art form, and you may want to hire this out at least for the first few releases until you get a feel for the best way to present them.

I have listed some online Press Release resources in Appendix C.

Avoid Large Packages of Backlinks

Do not buy packages that purport to sell you hundreds of automatic backlinks. Backlinks are best if regularly added over a period of time. Many backlinks at once may get you a rise in the rankings, but it will be short lived and will be harder to rank in the future.

This is not an area to rush. It is much more effective as a long term campaign.

CHAPTER 6
USING FACEBOOK

I debated not including a section on social media, because it could almost be an entire book in and of itself. Furthermore, getting involved in social media (such as Facebook) before you have your website optimized is akin to putting the cart before the horse.

A Facebook Business Page can be set up to help give your business greater exposure, but it should never be a replacement for your actual website, and your website should be fully up to speed before you start using social media as a resource.

With that in mind, I am going to cover just a few very basic items about integrating Facebook into your business plan.

One thing to keep in mind when using Facebook is that according to the Terms of Service they own the rights to everything you publish on their site. Do not put proprietary information on any Facebook site and do not post any content there in which you need to retain full copyright. Other than that, you can have a lot of fun with it, while at the same time using it to get more customers.

Facebook, the internet's largest social networking site was originally created to stay in touch with friends and share recommendations. In that context, the 'Like' feature is a casual way of expressing a personal preference and telling your friends about something new.

For a business owner, collecting a lot of "Likes" can translate into real dollars and have a positive impact on the success of your company.

Here are a few tips on how to gather those "Likes" for your Facebook Business Page.

1. Compile a list from your personal and professional email address books - not just customers, but also business associates and acquaintances. Send an announcement that you put up a Facebook Page for your business and would like some honest feedback and suggestions. Ask them to "Like" it if they appreciate what they see.

2. Offer an incentive. Bribes are time-tested marketing tools! People love getting something for free. Offer a free report, a discount coupon or some other "legal bribe" in exchange for "Liking" your Business Page. Just make sure that the freebie you offer is something your target market finds valuable and can actually use. Free reports that offer solutions to your customers' common problems can be helpful not just to get the "Like" but also to let them know you are more than capable of helping them with their needs.

3. Add the "Like Box" widget to your blog or website. This can be found by entering the appropriate information at: developers.facebook.com/docs/reference/plugins/like-box This widget streams your Facebook Business Page to your website and allows visitors to "Like" it without having to actually visit Facebook. It also displays a selection of fan avatars so your visitors can see some of your current friend-base. The easier you make it for people to "Like" your page, the more "Likes" you'll attract.

When utilizing Facebook, be prepared to spend a bit of time managing it. If a customer posts a message on the site praising one of your products and no one from your company ever comes back to say, "Thanks" then it is quite possible that customer could feel slighted. That would have the exact opposite effect you are going for.

Avoid the use of automated software when using Facebook. You can hire someone to do this for you, but as was mentioned in a previous chapter, posting on FaceBook is best done by you or one of your workers that interacts frequently with the customers.

Some business owners are afraid of Facebook because it gives customers an opportunity to post negative feedback. In reality, if someone posts something negative, it is a great opportunity to show off your excellent customer service. You can turn it around to regain the trust of the customer who left the negative comment as well as let other potential customers get a first hand glimpse at your professionalism and willingness to please your customers.

That is enough information to allow you to at least get your foot in the door with Facbook, but allow me to reiterate that I put this as the last chapter because you need to have everything on your main business website up to speed and fully optimized before taking on social media.

CONCLUSION

Although everybody wants good listings, there are unfortunately many sites that rank poorly or not at all. In many cases this is because they have failed to consider how a search engine works.

In particular, they forget that submitting to search engines is only part of the equation when you are trying to get a good search engine ranking for your site. While it is important to prepare your site through Search Engine Optimization, you cannot forget Site Optimization.

This ensures that the pages of your site are accessible to search engines and are focused in such a way that they will help improve the chances of them being found by the search engine spiders.

Of course, the most important thing to remember is your visitor and why they are there. Provide them with what they need in an informative, interesting, engaging way. Be sure they can find you in the search engines and you are off to a well-ranked site.

A site with good search engine listings is likely to see a dramatic increase in the traffic that it receives, especially if you have done the proper keyword and market research.

See you in the Search Engine Results Pages! Get More Customers!

APPENDIX A
WEB DIRECTORIES

When submitting to directories, make sure you are in the right subtopic (drill down as deep as you can get within the categories provided). Some sites will let you submit interior pages and some will only let you submit the home page. Pay attention to the rules. Also, don't spam keywords – choose them wisely using proper research techniques. For the description, use your Meta Description if it has been properly optimized.

A small sample of Free Directories:

Open Directory Project   http://www.DMOZ.org

Jayde   http://www.Jayde.com

So Much   http://www.SoMuch.com

DMEGS   http://www.DMEGS.com

There may be industry-specific directories for your company. You may either search for them on the net or ask a good SEO company to locate some for you.

A small sample of Paid Directories:

Many people will recommend Business.com as a directory. It may help with rankings – for now. I do not like their business model, and do not submit to them unless a client demands it. Use your own discretion.

There are other paid directories, and there may also be industry-specific ones that might be suitable for your business.

Yahoo! Directory   https://ecom.yahoo.com/dir/submit/intro/

Best of the Web   http://BOTW.org/

Aviva   http://www.AvivaDirectory.com/

APPENDIX B
ARTICLE DIRECTORIES

Be sure to follow the guidelines from the book when submitting articles. I highly recommend using a Media and Content Publisher for article submission. I am not saying that to get more business, although I am taking on clients. Whoever you hire, just be sure to "look over their shoulder" and make sure they know what they are doing. This can be a huge boon to your business if done right.

There are literally hundreds of these sites. Below is just a small sampling of some of the better ones.

Ezine Articles	http://ezinearticles.com/
Go Articles	http://goarticles.com/
Articles Base	http://www.articlesbase.com/
Search Warp	http://searchwarp.com/
ISnare	http://www.isnare.com
Buzzle	http://www.buzzle.com
Web Pro News	http://www.webpronews.com

If using other directories, make sure they have a decent Page Rank prior to submission and follow the rules so you don't get banned or get your submissions rejected.

You may also find article directories that are only for a particular niche that will post industry-specific articles.

APPENDIX C
PRESS RELEASE WEBSITES

Here is a list of some of the best Press Release websites, both free and paid. I recommend trying your hand at some of the free ones before you pay any money to have a press release issued. As mentioned earlier, it is advisable to hire someone to write a few of these for you before doing it on your own, unless you have previous experience at writing press releases.

http://www.Free-Press-Release.com

http://www.PRLog.com

http://www.PR.com

http://www.OpenPR.com

http://www.1888PressRelease.com

http://www.24-7PressRelease.com

http://www.I-Newswire.com

APPENDIX D
RESOURCES

Feel free to visit the author's websites:

http://www.EdAkehurst.com provides online marketing tools and tips – it is geared more towards internet marketing, but there may be a few tips that would also apply to your business.

http://www.GetToNumberOne.com is the site for the author's SEO company, Oak Business Services. No business is too small or too large.

http://www.OakPublishingGroup.com is the Publisher of this book, and is the author's Media and Content Publishing Company.

APPENDIX E
GLOSSARY

Accessibility – Making a site more user-friendly to hearing and visually impaired visitors.

Alt Attribute Text (or Alt Text) – Designating a word or phrase in place of a picture for accessibility purposes. Also has SEO advantages.

Backlink – A link from another web site that "points back" to your web site. These are very important for SEO purposes, authority and credibility.

Blog – Colloquial term for "Web Log". A dynamic web site with constantly updated and changing content. Blogs are usually updated on a regular basis and are themed around a particular topic.

Boards – see *Forum*.

Browser – The software interface that allows you to view web pages on your computer. The most common browsers are Firefox, Safari, Chrome and Internet Explorer.

Content, Page (or Onsite Content) – The text and graphics on your web site.

Content, Offsite – Text and graphics about or related to your website, but that are placed elsewhere, such as on an article directory or in a blog.

Directory, Article – A directory resource containing articles. Article Directories are usually broad in topic, but some are industry-specific or niche-specific. These are a great place to put backlinks.

Directory – A listing of web sites. Directories can be broad in scope or topic-specific.

Frame – A window displayed within a browser. Usually a web site is one large frame, but some sites consist of numerous frames "pasted" together or nested within each other.

Forum – A website where people come together online to discuss a particular topic. Users can post information, sometimes as questions and answers, sometimes as informational posts. Forums are another great resource for backlinks.

Google Places – A feature of Google that lists local businesses.

H Tags – Header Tags. H Tags are a code within HTML. Identifies that the text within the tag is a header, ranging from 1 (large) to 6 (small). H Tags also serve an SEO function.

Header – A category or subject heading within a web page. Shows emphasis. Also refers to text or graphics at the top of a web page

HTML – HyperText Markup Language. A language used to code web pages so that the browser knows how and where to display text, graphics, forms, links, and other web page content.

HTML Editor – Software that allows an HTML web page to be designed or edited. Most are visual editors, so that users who do not know HTML can design a page.

Hyperlink – A word, phrase or image that can be clicked to take a web visitor to another site, another page or a place within the same document.

JavaScript – A language used to code web pages. Has more flexibility than HTML and is used to create dynamic web pages.

Keyword – A word commonly used in search terms that is specifically used in writing content so that the content closely matches what is being searched for by the end reader.

Keyword, Long Tail – A Keyword phrase that is more specific to a search term than one or two keywords alone and is used in optimizing content for less competition.

Keyword Research – The act of researching how much competition and popularity a particular keyword or keyword phrase has while discovering its commercial viability.

Link, Inbound – A link from another website, pointing to your website.

Link, Outbound – A link from your website pointing to another web site or (sometimes) to another page within your website.

Link Structure – The structure used to design and place links for SEO and usefulness. Incorporates placement, anchor text, keywords and other factors.

Link Text (or Anchor Text) – The text on or near a hyperlink. For SEO purposes, the text will be relevant to the topic or theme of the page to which the link points.

Media and Content Publisher – A Publisher of media and content for the purposes of website visibility. Handles backlink strategies through the publication of relevant and strategically placed articles, press releases, posts, and other content, primarily (but not always) off site.

Meta Description – A Description of the page within the Meta Tags. Not seen on the site, but used by some Search Engines as the description in the SERPs.

Meta Keywords Tag – A Meta Tag containing relevant keywords used in the page for which the Tag applies. Not thought to have much SEO value, but used nonetheless.

Meta Tag – A Tag within the HTML of a webpage that reveals relevant information about the page that is not seen by the web site visitor.

Pay Per Click Advertising – A form of advertising where the advertiser pays a fee every time a user clicks on the ad.

Page Rank – A numerical designation used by Google to determine the quality and popularity of a web site, ranging from 0 - 10.

Rank – The weight a Search Engine gives a web site based on particular keywords or keyword phrases. The higher the rank, the closer to the top of the SERPs.

Search Engine – Software that finds relevant websites based on search terms entered by a user.

Social Media – Websites and content designed for social interaction. Prominent sites are FaceBook and Twitter.

Submission, Article – The act of submitting an article to an article directory.

Submission, Site – The act of submitting a site to a site directory or a Search Engine.

Page, Dynamic - A web page that changes based on user input.

Page, Internal - A web page that is not the home page.

Page, Static – A web page that does not change based on user input. Most web pages are static and are written in HTML.

SERP – Search Engine Results Page. The output of a search engine after having located relevant websites based on search criteria input by a user.

Search Engine Robot – see *Search Engine Spider*

Search Engine Spider – Sent out by a Search Engine to crawl websites and return relevant information that can be sorted and used in determining ranking based on relevance of future search terms.

Search Engine Optimization – The act of optimizing a web site for the purpose of achieving higher rankings. Includes onsite and offsite optimization techniques.

Site Optimization - The act of optimizing a web site for the purpose of achieving higher rankings and greater readability and usability. Includes onsite optimization techniques, and is mostly geared towards the end user, rather than towards a Search Engine.

Title Tag – The Tag that lists the Title of the web page. Will display at the top of the window of most browser programs.

URL – Uniform Resource Locator. An address for a website. When the address is typed into a browser, the web page is viewable by the user.

ABOUT THE AUTHOR

Ed Akehurst lives on the Mason Dixon line. He makes a living doing SEO, building websites, and publishing and distributing media and content. He has a wife, two children and the occasional rescued guinea pig.

www.ingramcontent.com/pod-product-compliance
Lightning Source LLC
Chambersburg PA
CBHW051241170526
45165CB00004B/1530